GIVING UP IS NOT AN OPTION

by

CHARLES MOORER JR.

PUBLISHED BY BLUE ARTISTS, LLC

Copyright © 2016 Charles Moorer Jr.

All rights reserved. Published by Blue Artists, LLC

Printed in the United States of America

This publication may not be reproduced, stored in a retrieval system, or transmitted in whole or in part, in any form or by any means, electronic, mechanical, photocopying, recording, or otherwise, without the prior written permission of Charles Moorer Jr. or Blue Artists, LLC, the representing agency. To order additional copies of Giving Up Is Not An Option please visit charlesmoorerpraise.com

This publication is designed to provide accurate and authoritative information in regard to the subject matter covered. It is sold with the understanding that the publisher is not engaged in rendering legal, accounting, or other professional service. If legal advice or other expert assistance is required, the services of a competent professional service should be sought.

*This book is dedicated to my wife Crystal, and my children Chelsea, and Chadwin.
We have been so blessed to overcome so much for such a time as this. As I share with others our intimate story of hope, encouragement, and overcoming, let this always be a reminder of how God kept his arms around us and planned this moment in our lives. I love you very much and thank God for all of your love, support, and understanding.*

A SPECIAL NOTE TO READERS

Finally to the readers of this book, my hope is that as you read this book you will be inspired, motivated, and encouraged, realizing that you are not alone with the struggles you go through. You can and will overcome if you put into practice Philippians 4:13. Remember your struggles may be real but so is God!!!

WHEN LIFE GETS TOUGH HOW DO I HOLD ON?

Then Job arose, and rent his mantel, and shaved his head and fell down upon the ground and worshipped, and said naked came I out of my mother's womb, and naked shall I return thither: the Lord gave , and the Lord hath taken away; blessed be the name of the Lord. In all this Job sinned not, nor charged God foolishly.

Job Chapter 1:20-22

ACKNOWLEDGEMENTS

With special thanks:

- To my siblings, Charlotte, Carry, Christ and Cheryl, the greatest gift our parents gave to us is one another. Your prayers, encouragement, support, and love is appreciated. Love you guys.

- To the members of Charles Moorer and the Faithful Few music ministry, singers and musicians, your understanding commitment, prayers, encouragement, has just been amazing! Your support is sincerely appreciated.

- To the Divine Direction Christian Church Family, I appreciate your support, and for allowing me to just be myself as the senior pastor of the Divine Direction family. Through the years we have gotten so much accomplished and have been a blessing to so many people. I look forward to our being a blessing to many more!

- To the Indiana Riley Children's Hospital medical staff; Dr. Batra, Dr. Rouse, Dr. Lazarus, support team and nurses, words cannot describe how my family and I feel about your genuine caring and concern that went well beyond the call of duty. We thank you over and over.

- To the Indiana Make A Wish Foundation, the love and care that you show so many children and their families throughout Indiana is just amazing! I look forward to doing what I can to assist the Indiana foundation with continuing to fulfill its mission of making kids dreams become reality.

- To the Florida Give The Kids The World Village, what a beautiful place of refuge for children and their families. A special thanks to the entire staff and volunteers for making our stay so special.

CONTENTS

Chapter 1
The Impact of Difficult Situations — p 1

Chapter 2
The Perils of Job — P 5

Chapter 3
Hard Times Do Not Discriminate — p 9

Chapter 4
The Rise To A Better Life — p 13

Chapter 5
A Change of Heart and Mind — p 17

Chapter 6
Challenging Times — p 23

Chapter 7
Daddy, I Have Faith — p 31

Chapter 8
The Battle To Overcome Cancer — p 33

Chapter 9
The Need for God's Reassurance   p 43

Chapter 10
Another Unexpected Crisis   p 47

Chapter 11
Life Started to Shine Again   p 53

Chapter 12
Celebration of Life   p 57

Chapter 13
Another Test of Faith and Trust   p 61

Chapter 14
Restored With A Desire To Give Back   p 67

Giving Up Is Not An Option

by
Charles Moorer Jr.

Chapter One
The Impact of Difficult Situations

HOW MANY TIMES in your life have you had to contend with difficult circumstances or situations that simply made you want to throw your hands up and walk away? If you said never, I would question your response. You see it is not uncommon for people every day around the world to face challenges in their lives, both directly and indirectly. For example, you have worked for a company for twenty-five years of your life. Your goal is to retire from the company, have quiet days, and just indulge yourself with the opportunity to do something you have always wanted to do. Sounds really good! However, you need at least five more years to get to that magic thirty years of service. By the way, prior to retiring, you are ok with the additional five years of working as you have a few financial housekeeping issues that need to be taken care of, and you cannot afford for those issues to be resolved out of your retirement income. The bottom line is that you have mapped out a good game plan for the next chapter of your life.

One day, you are on the job doing what you typically do throughout your work day, and have plans after work to go car shopping with your spouse. Suddenly, your supervisor walks toward your desk, like he has done for the last twenty-five years, for a casual conversation. However, you notice the expression on his face does not reflect a day that is going well for him. Out of concern and because of your twenty-five year relationship with him, when the supervisor gets to your desk, you plan to make sure he's ok. As soon as the supervisor gets to your desk, you stand with a smiling face to welcome him. But just as you prepare to do so, the supervisor tells you he has some difficult news to share with you and proceeds to tell you that the company is downsizing, and your position has been eliminated, effective immediately. In addition, the company has asked that you leave the premises that very moment. Security then escorts you out of the building,

GIVING UP IS NOT AN OPTION

and you are no longer considered an employee of the company. How would this make you feel?

Perhaps this is not an example you can relate to so let's try another one. Both of your parents are alive. However, one of them suffers from Alzheimer's, while the other struggles to take care of him. You reflect on how strong and vibrant your parents once were. How they were a blessing not just in your life, but also in the lives of so many others. Unfortunately, you are now watching the struggles they are having. It pains your heart to see that your father can't remember much while your mother, whose love is unconditional, struggles to care for him. Since your financial resources are limited, there is only so much you can do. Nevertheless, it is your mother that is taking on so much of the responsibility, and you can tell the caregiving is wearing on her. These are your parents, who have loved and cared for you, protected you, looked out for not only their immediate family, but have also poured their time and energy into the lives of other people. Even if it was not always appreciated, they still continued to help others. The thought of the entire situation is very painful. How would this make you feel?

While these are just a few examples, the point is that we can all relate to these situations on some level. More importantly, if we are not careful, the situations and circumstances of our lives can cause us to give up.

The employee, who was forced out of a job, the spouse, and child in our Alzheimer's example, could all be broken and disheartened by these situations. How? As you consider this, you will notice there are a wide range of variables to consider and that these considerations are relevant to some of the issues you may have encountered in your life. The examples provided are certainly relevant to my life, and I will share those experiences with you a little later on. However before doing so, let's examine a story that goes back thousands of years and is still relevant to the mindset of giving up versus not giving up.

Chapter Two
The Perils of Job

IN THE BIBLE, there is a story about a man named Job. The story of Job seems to focus on the following points: Why would a good and faithful person have to suffer tragedies if all suffering is caused by human sin? And does God cause people to suffer? And if so why?

At the end of the story we are taught that the mysterious ways of God are sometimes beyond human understanding, but that the presence of God with us in times of suffering can give us the strength to go on and face the future. But that still does not mean that going through the trials and tribulations we have will not weigh heavily on us, causing us to want to give up at times.

According to the Bible, Job was a good man who feared, and respected God. He refused to indulge in things that were not right. In fact, Job would get up daily to pray forgiveness for his seven sons and three daughters, who appeared from the story to enjoy partying, just in case they did anything to offend God. Also, he was considered a very wealthy man as he owned seven thousand sheep, three thousand camels, five hundred oxen, five hundred donkeys, and a large number of servants. The important thing to remember here is that in ancient times, people often believed that riches, a large family, and good health, were signs of favor from God. From reading the story, it appeared that Job had all these things and was the richest man for miles around. However, as we read on we find that the comfortable lifestyle and pleasures that Job had become accustomed to had all been suddenly taken away. Does this sound familiar?

Rest assured you are not alone as there are many people who can sincerely appreciate this part of the story. One of the key components of this particular story has to do with how Job lost everything. As the story goes, it all started with Job being robbed, followed by the murder of his servants, robbery, murder of more servants, and then ultimately a catastrophic windstorm that caused the residence of his oldest son to collapse and fall on all ten of Job's children, who happened to be at the oldest brother's home partying, killing them all. To complicate matters further, Job's health took a toll for the worse, and his wife became discouraged, frustrated, and hopeless, advising Job to just give up by cursing God and die. We should point out that at times, the wife in this story is not always understood for her position. However, we should be mindful that a mother losing a child can be a devastating experience for any woman.

This is something that my wife and I experienced with our first child. My wife was diagnosed with a severe case of Preeclampsia. In brief, this condition occurs when you're pregnant and have high blood pressure and protein in your urine. It can happen at any point after week 20 of pregnancy. This condition is also called toxemia, or pregnancy-induced hypertension (PIH). It only occurs during pregnancy, but it can occur earlier than week 20 in some cases. This medical condition caused our child to be born prematurely. Unfortunately, the child lived long enough for my wife to get well and then went home to be with the Lord. While we have since had other children, it has taken many years for my wife to recover mentally and emotionally.

The point is that Job's wife lost all of her children as well, and so you can only imagine what was running through her mind. Also, she watched her husband's health severely deteriorate. It would appear that the loss of the material possessions did not mean nearly as much as the loss of her children and the suffering of her husband. In simple terms, her family had been taken, and that penetrated her heart. We can make this assumption, in part, because only after Job was afflicted in his body, did his wife advise him to give up by cursing God and dying.

CHAPTER THREE

HARD TIMES DO NOT DISCRIMINATE

WHEN WE EXAMINE the concept of giving up versus not giving up as told through this biblical story, we must examine Job's state of mind through his time of trial and tribulation, as it is still relevant today. Job wished that the day of his birth was blotted out; Job asked, "why didn't I die before birth?" Job asked, "why does God let me live?" Job asked, "what did I do wrong?" Job asked, "why is life so hard?"Job finally concluded that he was "sick of life. "

Now let's just think about how many times life

has taken you to this same mindset. If you say you have never been there before, then good for you. However, I can assure you that at some point in your life, you may experience frustrations that will likely cause you to have some of the same mental challenges reflected by Job some thousands of years ago before our time.

The good news is that this is normal. Yes, this is normal. Why? Human beings love being in control of situations and circumstances especially when those situations or circumstance might have a profound impact on their lives. Let me say that when we examine the mindset of Job, we must first realize no matter how badly he felt, the bottom line was that he simply had done nothing wrong. His situation was not caused or created by anything he did or didn't do. There is no question that this fact alone would cause many of us going through trials in our live to toss in the towel and give up. Does that sound familiar?

Sometimes you just get sick and tired of being tired. This reminds me of a story shared with me by my mother regarding her own outlook on life. At one point, she felt that the circumstances and situations in her life were so trying that it was just not worth living anymore. Not just for her but for her children as well. One day, after reflecting on her life as she felt it was, my mother decided to lay my siblings and me across the bed to take a nap. Once we were asleep, my mother turned on the gas on the stove and then laid across the bed next to us with the intention of our never waking back up in this life. However, she did not realize that the door to the house was not locked. Her brother just happened to come by, open the door and walk in. This put an end to what could have been a very bad situation. For certain there was divine intervention taking place here. My mother told me that she could not thank the almighty God enough for intervening and allowing her another opportunity to focus on what was really important. The point is that in challenging times, no one is above feeling several of the negative emotions Job felt and giving up is something even the best of us are tempted to do from time to time.

As you'll soon find out, giving up is a mind set that does not discriminate based on money, power, looks, material possessions, relationships, health or other. One can have all of these things, some of these things, or none of these things, and still want to give up on your wife, husband, children, parents, siblings, career opportunities, and even on yourself.

Chapter Four
The Rise To A Better Life

LET ME SHARE a story with you that is very near and dear to my heart. It pertains to my own family.

With few exceptions, my wife and children have been blessed to experience many wonderful things. Given the fact that my wife and I never had much growing up, we had just been so grateful for everything God blessed us with throughout our lives as a married couple. While it is true that in the early years of our marriage we had very humble beginnings, over time, God blessed us to accomplish and experience a lifestyle we had never before been accustomed to. For example, we went from sitting and sleeping on the floor in our one bedroom apartment to building three homes. The memory of coming home from work to our one bedroom apartment and my wife as sweet as she could be preparing dinner for us using phone books as our dinner table is still fresh in my mind and is very sentimental to me. We had no furniture, so we just sat on the floor, ate and talked. There were struggles of finding a job to getting a pretty decent career and moving up in management fairly quickly. My income increased, and it was great to know that I could purchase my favorite cereal, Peanut Butter Captain Crunch, and actually afford it!

We were blessed to go from one car to two and three cars. This was nice on many fronts as I had many memories of praying that my car would not stall on me when I came to a stop at a red light. Good, properly-running vehicles were absolutely a new frontier for me and boy was I thankful! In fact, for many years throughout my career in management, I was blessed with the experience of getting a new vehicle where I had no payments and did not have to pay for gas. During the recession, years beginning around 2008, the price of fuel was extremely high, making it rather difficult for many to afford. So, my appreciation for this blessing was heightened. We were also blessed to take nice family vacations staying in many beautiful places.

This was certainly a far cry from when my wife and I first got married and took our honeymoon in Vegas, which was essentially our first vacation together. The car broke down, forcing me to conduct a bootleg repair to keep it running along with a standby supply jug of water in the back seat in case it ran hot again. Oh, I should also mention that I watched the thermostat the entire way to our destination while my wife was sweating profusely and doing everything she could to keep cool, which included sticking her foot out the window at one point. Overall, I was not so sure the foot thing was working out for her, but given the circumstances, I chose to keep silent about it and just keep watching the thermostat. By the way, there was no air conditioning in the car.

As previously stated, my wife had a severe case of toxemia. As a result, she lost our first child and almost lost her own life. In fact, at one point the doctors told the family to come see her because she was not going to make it. There were times I would go to my local church and just pray that God would allow her to live. And I am grateful that he did just that. After the ordeal, the doctors said we would never have any children, as my wife was a high risk for a repeat of the toxemia. However, God blessed us with two children, a girl and boy, three years apart with my wife having no complications. It was truly a blessing. In addition, God worked on me and taught me so many lessons as it pertained to having faith. Life was good!

Chapter Five
A Change of Heart and Mind

ULTIMATELY, I CAME to know God on a completely different level from what I was taught growing up, and in a way that I had never truly thought that one could know Him. Essentially, I got to know Him for myself and not through what others told me. My relationship was simply based on the fact that I knew there were so many things in my life that I had no control over. Yet somehow, some way, through the good, bad, and the ugly, I was still standing. I knew there was something or someone beyond me that appeared to be guiding my life and the life of my family. My praying and reading the word of God contributed to my understanding of who he was but not necessarily his complete will for my life. Nevertheless, I grew to really appreciate and love and respect him, not for material things but because I realized he really cared for me. My desire to serve him and be a blessing to others letting them know that Jesus Christ is real and that he loves them became strong. Over time I became a minister in the church. Then I worked as a minister of music and started a music ministry called the "Faithful Few" with the goal of doing as much outreach as I could. For example, the group played in and out of state, at charity functions, in prisons, in senior centers, and anywhere we might have been needed and never charged a single dime. Several years later, when my dear friend, brother, and confidante, pastor Reginald Fletcher passed away, I found myself stepping into the role of senior pastor of Divine Direction Christian Church, formerly known as Northside Wesleyan. This was challenging in part because I continued to work a full-time job in corporate management. However, remembering where the Lord brought me from kept my focus on the goal of continuing with the goal of doing the job I believed God had called me to do. Financially, God had blessed me such that I did not need a salary from the church and was able to have the church utilize this to its advantage in helping with various programs

GIVING UP IS NOT AN OPTION

to assist others in need in and around the community. This was extremely important during the recession as there were so many people that had come through the church with needs and we were thankful that we could help. Throughout all of the work in ministry, my wife and children were very supportive. In fact, for the most part, other than the prison ministry, my wife and children traveled with me to performances to assist the sick and shut in, serve food to the community, volunteer in a homeless shelter, give away Christmas food and toys to others in need, and to allow me to be the best I can be at serving the God, who had been so good to us.

There is one thing that is important to realize. God Almighty is a God of order and not of confusion. A man that does not take care of his own home cannot serve God or his people properly. The basis of my reminding those who serve in the church of this very important biblical concept is so that you get the full blessings of the Lord in your life, starting in your home. Remember the old saying "charity begins at home then spreads abroad?" During my service to others, I did not neglect spending quality time with my wife and children. For example, I made time to participate in our children's school sporting and musical events, go to parent-teacher conferences, take the family out to the movies, have pizza night, take regular vacations with the family, cut my son's hair, listen and learn about their issues in school, play board games with my kids, and so many other things. Also, when it was time for my daughter and son to go to college, my wife and I were there to take them on school visits and make sure all of their needs were met, not only to attend college but to succeed as well.

My point is that one's service in ministry has more credibility when you live a life that is reflective of what you preach and teach, not just for those outside of your home, but for those in your home. No matter what, I wanted my family to know that I not only loved them but considered them a precious gift from God that required just as much of my attention.

For those of you who have never committed to ministry but intend to, you will soon find out that ministry done properly can be very tiring. You see, dealing with a wide variety of people and personalities can sometimes weigh heavily on your shoulders as you will often find yourself caring the burdens of others. For example, having performed several eulogies for many families over the years, no matter how my heart pains for them, often times there are no words I could truly say that would ease the pain being felt by those experiencing the loss. Sometimes, the situations were so painful that I thought about throwing in the towel. However, I realized that God would simply throw it back out at me.

So the love, support, and understanding of the

family God has entrusted you with are critical and can inspire you not to give up during the many challenges that will certainly come at some point in your life.

Chapter Six
Challenging Times

AS PREVIOUSLY STATED things were going pretty well for our family and life was good. While we were not rich with money, we were rich in spirit and, as stated, God had brought us a long way in terms of the quality of our life. However, things in our life would take a sudden twist and would challenge the very foundation upon which we were standing.

In 2011 my son, who was sixteen years old at the time, went to the driving range with me to hit a few golf balls. As he swung at the ball, I laughed very hard.

The more he swung, the harder I laughed. I laughed because every time he swung at the ball it looked like he was swinging at snakes! It was so incredibly funny! We concluded our day with a drink of cold water and went home. Several days later my son complained of pain on his right side, which, to me at least,was obviously from his swinging at snakes several days prior. I thought he had simply strained a muscle. We gave him some over the counter medicine to ease the pain, and it seemed to work. Some time went by and my son, who was also participating on his high school football team, continued going to football practice and playing in games. At some point, he complained again, and we gave him some more over the counter medicine, thinking his strain did not quite heal all the way. Some more time went by, and it appeared everything was fine. My son continued to play football. However, one week his team had games back to back. He was pretty excited about getting more playing time as he had trained hard all summer long and it appeared his hard work was paying off. We watched in awe as he played one Tuesday night. He ran down another player from the opposing team, stopping the player from scoring a touchdown. What a play and what an amazing night. I was so happy for my son!

However, that same night, I noticed that he had taken two hits in the back on his right side. My wife was not too thrilled about it, but he appeared ok and simply walked off the hits. That night after the game, we were in the car driving home and he was so excited about the game he had just played that he kept on talking about it. It was a good evening. Unfortunately, in the coming days, he began to complain of pain in his right side. This was where he had taken the hits during the game. This time the over the counter medicine did not appear to work, and the pain seemed more severe. I took him to a local clinic where a doctor performed x-rays. The x-rays looked normal, and the diagnosis was gas related. The hospital prescribed Prilosec OTC. But over the coming days, there was no improvement, and his condition became worse.

Now I have always been a bi-vocational, non-paid pastor. Just months before this issue, I worked for a company that was short staffed, causing me to work seven days a week often. I can remember delivering a Sunday sermon then rushing home to eat and then rushing to the office to work. It was really difficult. Over time, I thought it over and decided that I was no longer going to work with the company as it was impacting my health. After praying, I decided to walk away from the job and felt that I would simply get another one. However, in speaking with a dear friend of mine, he encouraged me to step out to start my own business. He then assured me that he would assist me with getting set me up with an office in a building he owned, and reminded me the worst that could happen was I not succeed and have to go back to the corporate world. This sounded good, but I was not sure this was the correct thing for me to do. Therefore, I needed more time to think things through. The good news was that over the years I had saved money so I knew my family would be ok.

Before finalizing my decision, my family and I traveled to Hershey Pennsylvania for some rest and relaxation. On the way back from our trip, I can remember looking at the beautiful scenery along the highway and thinking about what my friend said to me. The thought began to weigh heavily on my mind, and I came to the conclusion that starting my own business was the right thing to do. When I arrived back to Indianapolis, Indiana I proceeded with setting up in my friend's office. While it was exciting, it was also a period of anxiety as I was starting from scratch with no clients, not a whole lot of money for business, no staff, no 401k, and I had to buy a medical plan that would cover my family. Nevertheless, I had my faith and figured that if it was God's will, then the business would make it. Along the way, I remember getting employment calls from other companies. Just to be sure I was doing the right thing, I would investigate the companies. However, the strangest thing would happen in that when a company would ring my phone off the hook and I would reach out to them, I would never hear from them again. This happened several times and was one of

GIVING UP IS NOT AN OPTION

the oddest things I had ever experienced. There was no doubt in my mind that God was sending me a message to move forward and stay focused with the plan of starting my own business. Again, if God is truly driving the bus in your life, he owns the consequences of whatever he calls you to do. With this thought in mind, I became more comfortable and accepting of my decision.

During the process of setting up my business I needed to switch medical coverage, and so I did. My medical benefit plan was in place but due to some mix-up with the application, the coverage would not take effect for a few weeks. We were for the most part always a healthy family. What would a few weeks mean? We would soon find out those few weeks did make a difference. You see as previously stated, my son was in a great deal of pain. Therefore, we elected to take him to our family doctor. My wife arranged the appointment and took him to the office. During the examination, the doctor concluded based on the symptoms that the issue may have been with my son's gallbladder. The good doctor ordered an ultrasound, saying that an ultrasound would reveal the issue.

Given the circumstances with the medical coverage, the doctor advised waiting a week to have the ultrasound would be ok while my son took something for the irritation. My wife called me at work to explain the doctor's recommendation of getting an ultrasound of the gallbladder alone and that waiting another week should not cause any additional issues. Funny thing, the night before my son's appointment, my son was in a lot of pain. I remember trying to console him, but somehow I could just tell this was no ordinary pain he was feeling. While I was giving my son our usual fist bump and "love you" before going to bed, he gazed at me as though to say, daddy, please make the pain stop. While looking back at him, I reassured him that he did not have to worry, and that we were going to get him all better. Therefore, waiting another day for our medical benefits to begin so that we could have an ultrasound was simply not an option. With this in mind, my wife proceeded to take my son to get the ultrasound, and we paid cash to get it done. The technician, per the doctor's orders, was supposed to only look at the gallbladder and then come back in another week to perform an ultrasound on the kidneys. However, the technician went further and decided to look at the kidneys. The results were given to my wife who then called me up frantic and in tears. The ultrasound revealed my son had renal medullary carcinoma, or right kidney cancer. As I tried to calm my wife, the first thought in my mind was to call the doctor to get a better understanding of the findings. I wanted to hear it for myself. After calming my wife down as best I could, I phoned the doctor. The doctor spoke with me and explained the condition and was certain as was diagnosed. However, the doctor stressed the need for more testing. The doctor then apologized to me for the bad news.

Chapter Seven
Daddy, I Have Faith

REMEMBER, AS PREVIOUSLY mentioned, sometimes in difficult situations there are just no words that can provide the type of comfort you need. Sometimes no matter how much individuals tell you they understand, they really don't. As I spoke with the doctor, it felt like the room was spinning, and my feelings were numb at best. No question this is not the type of news that a father would want to hear about his only son. I took a deep breath and knew I had to get home to my family and re-assure them that the God we serve still loved and cared for us and was able to do exceedingly and abundantly more than we could ever imagine.

When I arrived home, I entered the house and went upstairs. My wife was in our bathroom crying heavily. Again, I tried to calm her by giving her a hug and telling her that at this moment, with everything we had, we would need to be as strong as we could for our son. Now while I said this, I was reminded of our Job story from the Bible. Recall the devastation Job's wife must have felt at the loss of her children? How about what Job must have felt? After all, the Bible tells us that he prayed for the protection of his children daily. Let me just say this was a tough pill to swallow. After talking with my wife, I went to see my son. As he sat on the couch, I asked him how he felt. My son looked at me and said: "Daddy I have Faith." I looked at my son and told him then we could work from there and reassured him that I would be with him every step of the way. We spoke some more about the game plan. At the end of our conversation, I stood up, and my son stood up with me. Tears began to flow from his eyes as he said: "Daddy I am so glad that you are here with me." I hugged my son and told him we would get through it.

Chapter Eight
The Battle To Overcome Cancer

IN ORDER TO understand the full significance of my son's diagnosis, one has to understand the type of cancer involved. So, what is renal cycle cell carcinoma?

Renal medullary cancer is a rare malignancy almost exclusively seen in young patients of African ethnicity. These patients often present with the cardinal symptoms of hematuria, flank pain, and an abdominal mass, and this malignancy has been associated with patients carrying the sickle cell trait. It is estimated that 300 million people worldwide carry the sickle cell trait, and the presence of hematuria in these patients should be treated as a harbinger of a possible malignancy. Notably, this tumor mostly develops on the right side of the body. Patients often present with it at an advanced stage, and the prognosis is poor. Therefore, a high index of suspicion in a patient of African descent presenting with a right-sided abdominal mass and hematuria may assist in an early diagnosis. Current chemotherapy options are very limited, and early detection may provide a chance for surgical resection. It may also provide a bigger time frame for the initiation of novel chemotherapy regimens in patients who fail current chemotherapy regimens.

Our family physician referred us to a doctor at Indiana's own Riley Children Hospital North where we met Dr. Sandeep Batra. My wife and I met with the doctor who explained the seriousness of the condition to us and advised the condition was rare and very unusual to see in a minor. In fact, the condition was so rare that the doctor conducted inquiries of other specialists in other states just to see what the recommended treatment for the condition was. Ultimately a treatment plan was developed. However, the doctor made us aware that there was no guarantee the treatment would work as there was typically a ten percent survival rate. The doctor further advised since my son was at stage three, we needed to move quickly as the doctor wanted to make sure the cancer had not

GIVING UP IS NOT AN OPTION

spread beyond the right kidney to other areas of the body. Accordingly, he scheduled a biopsy and bone scan. This took place at Riley Children's hospital downtown Indianapolis. Once the procedures were done, my son was going back to the north location to begin chemo treatments.

We took my son to the location, and he went through the prescribed procedure. While he was there, an interesting thing took place. One morning, my son had awakened to tell my wife and me about a dream he had. In this dream he shared with us, he sat on a horse with medieval armor on looking out over a cliff into a valley. There sat a man he described sitting on a dark horse with long stringy hair, wearing what appeared to be the same type of armor. The man appeared ready to fight against him. My son then looked over his shoulder to the rear and noticed myself, my wife, his uncles and aunts, his great grandmother, and other relatives all sitting on horses with armor prepared to assist him with the fight. However, when he looked back down into the valley, he noticed that there was not only the initial horseman, but there were hundreds more with him. My son and his family went down into the valley to fight, and as soon as he got to the valley, he was attacked by the enemy. While fighting the enemy, a man on a white horse that was much larger then anyone's horse, appeared next to him and began to fight alongside of him against the enemy. The man on the white horse had a large staff as his weapon. Whenever the enemy appeared to get to close, he would take the staff and waive it, striking the enemy down. Every time it appeared the enemy was going to overtake us, the man on the white horse would strike them down. What was even more fascinating to my son was that the enemy and his army did not attempt to attack the man on the white horse and appeared to want no parts of him. The enemy only wanted to attack us. The battle lasted a little while until there was no one else left to fight against us. My son said then he heard a voice say, "wake up, it's time to take your medicine." It was the hospital nurse. He was so excited about the dream and said he wished he could have stayed sleep a while longer to see what was going to happen next! As my wife and I listened, right away I understood what the dream stood for. When our family had learned of my son's condition, everyone, it seemed, went into prayer. My siblings drove from Akron, Ohio and showed up unannounced to be with us. Men from our church family came to my home unannounced to pray with us. Dr. John Loye, who is a preacher of the gospel, sent word through his wife that he was in Nigeria in the mountains fasting and praying for my son. So we had immediate and extended family interceding in prayer. However, the man on the white horse represented my lord and savior Jesus Christ's presence with my son and our family fighting against the enemy and his army. With tears in my eyes but joy in my heart, I knew that God was telling us that my son would have the victory and that he would survive the battle. There is a song that says the battle is not yours, it's the Lord's! This is why the dream ended with none of the enemies standing!

The point here is that when God tells you everything is going to be ok or that you will be victorious, he does not always provide you with a clear path on how that is supposed to happen. He just expects you to trust him, which is not always an easy thing to do. But I was reminded that the Lord said: "he will keep those in perfect peace whose mind is stayed on him because they trust in him" (Isaiah 26:3). Nice in theory, yet still not always easy to do. Nevertheless, if you are true believer, you don't really have a choice!

Once the biopsy was complete, my son was released from the hospital. Over the next few days, he seemed in better spirits and said, "daddy, I am going to beat it." I agreed. However, when we took him to start his first round of chemo, the doctor discovered that he had at least a liter of fluid in his lungs, and it needed to come out immediately. But since the tumor had gotten bigger, he also needed to start chemo. The order was placed, and my son went into outpatient surgery immediately to get a machine hooked up to him to start draining the fluid.

The chemo given to him was an aggressive type with the goal of shrinking the tumor. If the doctor could get the tumor to shrink, then the kidney would be removed. None of what we experienced over the next thirty days was planned. You see my son stayed in the hospital for that entire period. He became so weak from the treatments and all that he had been going through. I can recall helping him use the bathroom and him telling me how patient I was with him. Sometimes he even apologized for not being able to help himself. I reminded him that I was his father, and that I loved him and that it was my job and desire to look out for him. But, I also told him when I became an old man to make sure he was patient with me too! He smiled and said, "Daddy, when you get old, I will be there to take care of you, I promise!" I told him, "I am going to hold you to it!"

The good news was that after a few weeks, he came off of the machine that removed the fluid from his lungs. But he had been given so much chemo that he was extremely week. I can remember sleeping in the hospital, which I did every night, and him trying to get out of the bed to make it to the bathroom and falling or not making it in time. I would pick him up and take him, clean him up, clean up after him, and reassure him that everything was ok.

One night without warning, the medical staff burst into the room. The concern was that his blood pressure was out of whack. They asked him a lot of question about how he was doing and feeling, if he could breathe properly, and a host of other things. While I know they meant well, I was not thrilled with their entrance. That night had been one of the best nights he had. As I sat working, he had been speaking with his cousins on the phone and it was just so good to hear him feeling better and making jokes. He then got out of bed came over where I was sitting on the sofa bed and looked out the picture window behind me. As he gazed out the window, he said it seemed the world was passing him by. He then said, "daddy, I hope I get to graduate from high school, I hope that I can go to my prom, and I hope that I can go to college." I listened to him, then I told him, "son you will do all those things and more, just remember the dream God provided to you." We sat laughing. So you see when the doctors came in and created the stir, it made him anxious. I spoke with the doctors and explained how he was doing. They explained their thinking to me.

Once they were done, they decided to move him to ICU just to keep an eye on things. Once they felt comfortable that things were ok, they would move him back to a normal room. Once they moved him to the other room and things were quiet, I can remember him asking if everything was ok. I explained to him that everything was but that it was more convenient to have him in the ICU for the night. He would be moving out over the next day or two back to his original room. Then I told him to rest. As he laid there, I sat up with all of the lights off except the lights from the machines that were hooked up to him. With every beat of the heart rate machine I had thoughts running across my mind. My son looked over at me and said, "daddy is everything ok?" Again, I responded by telling him that everything was fine and to go back to sleep and get some rest. At about 8:30 am the doctors were having a staff meeting about my son and invited me. They went over all of his vital signs and everything appeared normal. However, someone observed that he was so weak and this was my cue to explain that from the beginning of the issue, my son had no rest and that if he was going to have more chemo he just simply needed to have rest. The doctors and staff listened and came up with a game plan to administer medicines while allowing him still to get rest. In addition, that morning Dr. Batra came to the room to check on him and I explained the issue. Ironically, the doctor informed me that my son could take a short break from chemotherapy at that point as the tumor had stopped growing and apparently, the chemotherapy was working.

The doctor said that they would allow him to rest and then pick it back up. This was the turning point as he rested up and was able to regain some strength. He later went back to the treatments. However, the treatments were just so hard on him that he could never seem to take all of the recommended doses of chemo.

This caused some concern for the doctor. One day the doctor was talking to me about how people are different and that some medical treatment may work for one person and not work for another. As we walked through my son's ordeal, the conversation shared between me and the doctor would come back.

One day the doctor was expressing his concern about my son not being able to take all of the treatment and I reminded him that no two people are the same and that despite the fact that my son could not take all of the recommended treatment, his body still responded. I then told the doctor that he was a man of medicine and I was a man of faith and that the two could work together. Doctor Batra was one of the most humble medical professionals I had ever met. He did not say he knew what was best, or that he has seen many children so don't tell him how to do his job. He simply said, "let me think about our next move. We will figure this out." This was a serious sign of humility, not arrogance, and I was so thankful that God chose him to be the instrument for such a time as this.

Chapter Nine
The Need for God's Reassurance

REMEMBER THE DREAM my son had?

As time went by, so much happened with my son that I started thinking heavily about the dream and questioning what it really meant. There was no question that I thought I had a pretty good grip on its meaning. However, I was so tired of watching my son struggle and the impact it was having on my wife and daughter that I just needed the lord to reassure me. Let me say that it is ok for us to ask for reassurance from God. The Bible story of Gideon is a great example of being able to ask God for this accommodation (Judges Chapter 6). You will notice that even though Gideon asked multiple times, God was patient with him and granted his request. There is no doubt in my mind that God's assurance any time, can give you the strength you need to stand in the midst of storms in your life.

With reassurance in mind, one night while lying on the hospital chair in my son's room, it was dark, he was sleeping and I could hear the sound of the hospital monitor, with so much on my heart and mind, I could not sleep. Taking a towel I went over to the side of my son's bed, folded the towel multiple times and placed it on the floor. I then got on my knees and begin to pray, asking God to reassure me of the meaning of the dream my son shared with me. After praying for some time, I got up and went back to the chair and went to sleep. Early that morning, there was a knock at the door. It was one of the doctor's administrative persons who made their way over to my son's room. Opening the door there stood the assistant who politely said, "hello someone is here to see you." There stood a tall Caucasian man who identified himself as the father of a child who recovered from having cancer. He then looked at me and said: "hello I am Aden's dad and just like my son survived yours will too. Prayer works." Immediately, I reached out to him, hugged him and began to cry. You see I knew that God had answered my prayer and provided me with the reassurance I was

GIVING UP IS NOT AN OPTION

seeking and needed. The gentlemen then came into the room, and as I asked my son to wake, the gentleman stood at the foot of the bed introduced himself as Aden's dad and just like his son, he would survive and told him "prayer works." He then handed my son a computer tablet to pass the time and left the room. As my son looked at the tablet, he asked me if I knew the gentleman was coming to his room. I told him that I did not but told him, "son, prayer works." As he was full of smiles looking at his tablet, I went into the bathroom, looked in the mirror and just cried. Up to that point, all I could really think about was being strong for my family. So I never really let out what was pinned up inside of me until that moment. God is awesome!

Now I felt like I had a second wind, and although days and nights were still tough, I had the confidence needed to keep fighting and encouraging my son to not give up. Guess what? It worked! After being in the hospital for almost thirty days, one of those being my birthday, he made it home for Thanksgiving. My wife made dinner. It was just our family sitting at the table, grateful, joyful, and thankful for our family still being a family of four. I watched my wife and kids interact and I cannot begin to tell you what I felt in my heart. The moment for me was so overwhelming, all I could do was thank God!

CHAPTER TEN
ANOTHER UNEXPECTED CRISIS

UNFORTUNATELY IN THE coming days, my wife would receive some news that stunned us. The doctors found a cyst the size of a grapefruit on her ovary which meant that my wife more than likely had cancer. To be exact, it was sixty percent likely that she did. The doctor recommended surgery and advised the surgery would confirm what they believed. Once the surgery was over, the doctor would determine additional courses of treatment needed. You can only imagine how my wife felt. My wife went through high and low periods. After all, first our son and now she has medical issues. This was truly a difficult time. However, there was a silver lining. My son's doctor called me and told me it appeared the chemo had worked as the tumor on the right kidney had shrunk significantly. The doctor was so excited. However, the doctor said we needed to get the tumor out by removing the kidney. We needed to schedule surgery. The doctor then apologized and told us that the surgery could only be scheduled during Christmas week. I told the doctor he did not have to apologize as Christmas day in the Moorer household is everyday not once a year. I told my wife the news, and we were so excited although she was still concerned about her condition.

Have you ever heard of the old saying "timing is everything?" Or how about "there is a time for everything under the sun?" Well, remember how I shared the story of starting my business and purchasing benefits for my family? One of the benefits I purchased was life insurance for my wife. What was interesting was that prior to my wife finding out about her condition and the need for surgery, she had undergone and passed a physical examination, (which was part of the approval process for getting the insurance coverage) making her eligible for the coverage. With this in mind, I was confident that my wife did not have cancer. Those of you who understand the concept of insurance may understand my rationale. In my mind, this approval was

GIVING UP IS NOT AN OPTION

God letting me know that no matter what the doctor thought, my wife did not have cancer and she was going to be ok. After communicating this to my wife, we got the news that her surgery date was now scheduled. Ironically, the surgery was scheduled during the same week as my son's surgery. Talk about a challenge! You see, I had no one that I could lean on to assist me and my family. Our extended family lived in another state, and the timing was just not very good. By the way, when tragedy strikes it never schedules an appointment! The good news was that I would be traveling within the state to bring my daughter home from college, and she could help at least with her mother.

The day finally came for my wife to have surgery. That morning, I sat in the lobby reading my Bible preparing for the Sunday Christmas sermon and just praying. Afterwards, I did take some time out to read some sports news in USA Today. The doctor finally came out and extended his hand to shake mine and told me that everything was fine and there was no cancer involved. After a while, I went back to check on my wife to make sure she was ok. After sitting with her while, I went home to get my daughter to bring her back to the hospital. The game plan was for her to spend the night at the hospital with my wife while I prepared to take my son to the hospital for his five hour surgery the next morning. That is correct, my wife had her surgery on a Tuesday and my son had his surgery on a early Wednesday morning. The next morning, I took my son to the hospital. Doctor Rouse prepped me on how the surgery would go and what they hoped to accomplish. The doctor also told me that he would come out to see me for the purpose of providing updates. As my son prepared to go into surgery, I prayed then gave him our typical good night hand shake. As I sat in the waiting room, time went by and the doctor came out to share with me the surgery went well and there were no surprises. The doctor did point out when my son was first diagnosed there were some spots located in the chest area that were believed to be cancer that may have spread from the kidney issue. However, the doctor advised during surgery that the spots could not be located as they were not there. The doctor was so happy, and I was really grateful and relieved. As the doctor went back to get my son ready for the recovery room, I placed a call to a gentleman who God used to help my family financially.

Recall when I first learned of my son's condition the timing was not very good financially speaking. What was amazing though was that God already had a plan. We were told early on that my son would be the million dollar medical kid. Since our medical benefits had not begun from the onset, I had to pay money out of pocket for things like an ultrasound and some of the pills he needed to take. But I did not care. I figured that I knew what it was like not to have, so if I had to start over or become bankrupt to save my son's life, it was a done deal. But as stated, God had a plan. This gentleman who had helped me early on told me that he experienced the same thing with his stepson, who he was extremely close with. The gentleman went on to tell me today my son is now his son and that I should not worry as he was going to help me. Now what was fascinating was that I never met him face to face, only over the phone. Yet somehow God blessed our spirits to connect, and the gentleman was true to his word. When I shared the results of the surgery with him, he cried and I thanked him for his kindness.

Chapter Eleven
Life Started to Shine Again

WHEN I MET my son in the recovery room, it was as though nothing ever happened and that he had just taken a nap. My son was taken to his room doing extremely well. In the interim, I phoned my daughter to make sure my wife was ok and all was well. Later that week on Friday, my wife came home. I traveled to the hospital and brought my wife and daughter home, and I stayed home for a little while to make sure everything was ok. Then I traveled back to the hospital to be with my son. That Saturday, which was Christmas Eve, I traveled back to my home to see my wife and daughter and to also get clothes together to take back with me to the hospital. You see, I told the church that I would be there Sunday morning to deliver the Christmas sermon.

There is an old but true saying; Jesus is the reason for the season! Everything seemed to be calm and I was thinking it was going to be a silent and holy night. However, it may have been a holy night, but it certainly was not silent! While my son was sleeping in the bed and I was attempting to sleep in the chair next to him, the phone rang. It was my daughter telling me that my wife was having some setbacks. It appeared her bowels were not working properly, creating tremendous pain. My daughter was questioning if the ambulance should be called. My wife wanted to wait a little while longer. I told my daughter that I would call her back. Immediately, I hung up the phone and began to pray asking the Lord to touch my wife. As I sat there, my daughter called to tell me that everything was ok and my wife was doing much better. The lord had touched her body. Thank you God!

I was able to close my eyes for a few hours, get up, get dressed, and go to the church where I provided the Christmas message of hope through Jesus Christ. It felt odd as my family was not present, yet it also felt pretty good to know that they were well. One of the church members (who reminds me so much of mother), prepared a dish of food for my family so that I could

GIVING UP IS NOT AN OPTION

take it home. After leaving the church, I went to my house and took the food to my wife and daughter. We chatted briefly as I had to get back to the hospital. Upon arrival at the hospital, I ran into a young lady in wheel chair. As she cried, I reached out to her to find out what was wrong. The young lady told me she had cancer and had a set back and did not want to be in the hospital on Christmas day. As I saw the tears from her eyes stream down her face, I was truly moved. The best thing I could do is to let her know my son was in the same situation, but that the good news was that they were both still alive to see another day as Christmas is every day. I prayed for her and then went on to my son's room where he was now awake. His room was so calm. The doctor came in and stood at the foot of his bed and explained the results of his surgery. He told him that he would never have to have a surgery of this type again. On a side note, the doctor performing the surgery only works the Christmas day schedule every eight years and it turned out this Christmas was that eighth year. This is significant as eight in the Bible is the number for new beginnings.

The family finally made it home. I was really tired but grateful that everyone was ok. To keep some sense of normal, I had put up Christmas decorations around the house and while Christmas day may have passed, we still had a lot to celebrate! We exchanged gifts and it was nice. Now my daughter had an issue as she was not sure she would be able to go back to college because she was unable to get an additional scholarship. I wrote her a check to cover the balance owed. Finally, we were getting back on track!

Chapter Twelve
Celebration of Life

IN THE COMING months, my son was given a trip by the Indiana Make A Wish Foundation to the Give The Kids The World Village in Orlando, Florida which was part of a Disney trip. Now what was interesting was that we never looked at this as his last wish but a celebration of him overcoming and living not just life, but a long life.

We had been to Disney before on a family vacation, but obviously under a different set of circumstances and certainly not at the Give The Kids

The World Village. In simple, I had never heard of this village and it truly is a special place for not only the children that are sick, but their families too. The children and their families are spoiled with amenities, fun food, and fellowship with other children and families who can truly understand the circumstances.

My son and my family had a wonderful time. I watched my son and daughter ride everything they could get on. I just got joy watching, my wife was doing well and I was just tired mentally but so very thankful. While at the village, I decided to go into the chapel. What's neat about this chapel is that the colors are beautiful and it is so peaceful inside. As you sit on the bench and meditate, it's almost as though you can hear the prayers of so many before you. As I sat, there were no words that could describe how I felt. I looked around the small chapel and I noticed a book on a table so I decided to investigate it further. I walked over to the table and opened it. What I saw caused tears to flow like streams of water from my eyes. The book was made up of hand written notes to God by people who had come to the village from all over the world. The notes consisted of many desperate cries for help, dealing with loneliness, depression, pain, worry, concern, and emptiness. Some even said they just could not understand why this was happening to their child and their family. There were also written prayers by others who read the stories of those in agony. No doubt those that had written prayers for others were going through much of the same experiences. To me, that was powerful to see that others could put aside a few moments to consider others suffering above their own.

I picked up the pen, and I began to write how I felt, thanking God for all that he had done for my family. Later that day, my children went into the tiny little chapel. My daughter read the stories she cried, and was just so thankful that my son and my wife were alive.

CHAPTER THIRTEEN
ANOTHER TEST OF FAITH AND TRUST

NOW THERE IS one more little part to the story. Prior to going to Disney with my family, I was having issues with back pain which appeared to be related to my sleeping in chairs at the hospital for extended periods of time. Accordingly, I decided to visit with my doctor who, as part of the visit, decided I needed to have blood work to also check my PSA and a urine analysis. In short, the doctor got the results of my PSA and told me that it was elevated but still normal. Nevertheless, given my family history of prostate cancer, the doctor wanted me to have a biopsy. During the biopsy the doctor could not see anything and again I had no symptoms of any kind. However, when the results from the biopsy came back, they were positive, and I was diagnosed with prostate cancer.

Given all that my family had gone through, I felt that the timing to tell them was not good. It just seemed that it was better not to tell my kids as I had a son who was now doing very well and a daughter who was just going back to college. In thinking things over, I decided to tell my wife and schedule a visit between the doctor and my wife and I. You see the doctor had told me that since early detection of my condition was made, my cancer was a low risk. My thinking was to let the doctor explain that to my wife. This would put her mind at ease.

The doctor visit took place, and it was decided that I would have the prostate removed. However, that would not take place until mid to late August of 2012. I remember after my wife finding out she asked me how I felt. I told her everything was ok. She then asked me if I was hanging on by a thread. My response to her was that If God did not want me to know about the condition, he would not have made me aware of it. Since he did let me know, then he still has plans for me and I am not going anywhere anytime soon. Apparently, she seemed ok with my response we joked a little and called it a day.

When we got back from Disney, my wife and I were busy working with the school on getting my son prepared to go back to high school as well as getting my daughter ready to go back to college. Once we got this accomplished, I had the surgery. After the surgery was fully complete and I was released to go home, a few days later I made our children aware of my condition and reassured them that everything would be fine.

During a post-surgery follow up visit with the doctor, the doctor advised that he was a little off on the form of cancer. You see, during the surgery the doctor discovered the form of cancer involved was an aggressive form. Nevertheless, the doctor then said that the good news was that it had been removed. Turns out my decision to have it removed was definitely the right thing to do!

After the surgery there was still another issue to contend with. For some reason, I continued to have a PSA score. My doctor was really concerned. You see, when men have their prostate removed, there are typically no more prostate scores to report. The fact that I still had a score was alarming to my doctor. We agreed that I would go under a full body scan to rule out other possibilities. Pretty confident about my condition, I told the doctor that he was not going to find anything else, but that I would go through other tests as recommended. My thinking was that I had already been through so much with family and I was still standing. So there had to be a reason why God allowed this to happen in my life even if I could not understand why. After all, I tried to do everything I could to show God how much I appreciated everything he had done for me and my family. Even as my family went through so much, I may have gotten on my knees and just stayed there for long periods of time because the pain was so gut wrenching. There were no words to describe my feelings. I still never gave up the hope I had in the power of the living God.

In fact, I can recall a night where my music ministry The Faithful Few, had to perform in a concert. The commitment to participate in the concert was made months before our finding out about my son's condition. The night of the event, my son was still in the hospital. My wife asked if I would continue to minister to others that night. After all when you're going through your own challenges how do you encourage others to hang in there? My mind was made up in that I was going to show God that I trusted he was in charge. The night of the concert, we ministered to others. When the concert was over, we loaded the equipment and I went back to the hospital to stay with my son.

Three weeks after having my surgery, there was a slight schedule mix up with a guest speaker that was supposed to come to our church to speak. The speaker could not make it. So I figured it was meant for me to

GIVING UP IS NOT AN OPTION

stand in front of the congregation and deliver the message of the day. Without any complaining as the senior pastor of the church, I did my job. Therefore, no matter what the doctor told me about my PSA issues, based on my observations, I just did not feel God was through with me yet and I was not going to give up!

The scan was scheduled and the results were normal My urologists was still concerned and wanted to just keep me under observation. But he also felt that it might be good to consider some radiation treatments down the line. I agreed to the consultation. However prior to that consultation, I learned a little more about potential reasons for having a reading after prostate surgery, which consisted of the presence of cancer or even the presence of scare tissue after surgery. I then proceeded to have my PSA checked on a regular basis and noticed the scores begin to decline, going from a 0.80 to 0.24. Nevertheless, at the recommendation of my urologist, I proceeded with the radiation consultation. As I listened to the doctor explain the process I just did not get a good feeling about it. I shared with the doctor my recent PSA results and he seemed stunned. We agreed to have another test performed at a hospital. It was believed the hospital results would be more accurate than the local medical office or any walk in facility. My lower test results came from a reputable walk in clinic. Nevertheless, I agreed, and the doctor advised he would see me again to discuss the results from the hospital.

So, I had the test performed and had the follow up. Guess what? The hospital results agreed with my 0.24 and I declined radiation with the doctor also agreeing. My thought was that I certainly did not want to take radiation for a condition that I no longer had as this could create other problems. The funny thing is that my PSA has been as high as 0.80 and drop as low as 0.15 where it is to this day. My urologist tells me he cannot figure that out, but all is well!

Chapter Fourteen
Restored With a Desire to Give Back

ONE YEAR LATER my son would be running track for his high school and participating in the young men of purpose group. The group is made up of young men that serve others throughout the community. One of the things that was really touching was to see my son, one year from the day of having surgery, take toys and food to other families as well as running in a two mile race where he actually placed second in his group. As I drove down the road with him in the car from an event, he looked at me and said, "Daddy, it feels good."

Given all that he had been through, I understood, as it felt good for me to see him being a young spirited teenager again and cancer free.

By the way, my son went on to graduate high school on time, go to his prom, and on to college. He also went on to work as a youth counselor for the YMCA. What a blessing!

My wife decided that she would collect toys for the terminally ill kids at Riley Hospital, along with providing items for the parents and caregivers for the kids once a year. So we reached out to our church family, other organizations, and took money out of our pocket to get it done. One year it just so happened that there were nineteen beds in the hospital, and on Christmas Eve, every last one of those beds was filled with sick children. The nurses were so grateful that my wife and my daughter brought all of the gifts and told her they were going to wrap them up on Christmas Eve and place them at the foot of each child's bed so that they would see them in the morning.

My daughter went on to graduate from college with her bachelor's degree.

And me? The Lord blessed me and I did not have to go bankrupt or skip a beat financially in taking care of my family.

By the way, during the entire time, I never took a salary from the church. My business gained traction, allowing me to put myself on salary and start bringing in others to help. In addition, I continued with my music ministry, working as a senior pastor, and teaching as an adjunct professor, sharing my story with the students.

CONCLUSION

So what does this all mean? When you take a look at the story of Job, it reminds us that good people can experience difficult times. Nevertheless, how you go through those difficult times may determine how you come out of them. We should always remember that difficult times are not always triggered by something you may or may not have done. In those moments, instead of being angry with God, try trusting him. After all, what do you have to lose? If you are receptive to the concept of trust in action and not just in word, then you will also realize that your situation may go well beyond just you. Think about it, Job lost all that he had but refused to give up. In his mind, he still had to be the leader of what house he had left. We know for certain his wife was still in the picture. We also know that he had friends that were watching how he handled his situation. Thus, for those that remained, Job was still displaying powerful leadership through his example of perseverance and being steadfast in what he believed, while reminding others of his trust in the God he served. As the story goes, God overwhelmingly restored all that Job lost.

The story I have shared with you about my family struggle taught me this very important concept.

While I may not have been the richest man in the West, I was certainly appreciative, prayerful, practical about my service and belief in God, and always trying to make sure that I was staying in synch with what God wanted from me and my family. When I thought things over, I realized if I had not trusted God and decided to give up, what would that have said about me as a leader in my own home? How about in my own business? How about the ministries that I am involved with? There is an old saying that suggests "the best predictor of future leadership behavior is past leadership behavior in similar circumstances." Therefore, when times get hard and you give up, you may never know the far-reaching consequences of your decision and how it may impact others.

Let us not be fooled into thinking that every situation has a pleasant ending. For example, I have a friend named Jim. Jim lost his child, Mathew, to sickness. My friend was angry with God. Like Job, he feared God and tried to do as much good as he could. Yet his son's life was still cut short. The sting and pain of the loss made him understandably angry and bitter. One day Jim was sharing his feelings with the doctor. To his surprise the doctor asked him this question: "Jim would you have preferred that Mathew was the son of another father so that you would not have to feel the way you are feeling right now?" Jim said he paused and told the doctor, "absolutely not! Mathew was my son!" Jim then realized he should be thankful for the time he had with his son, as it was precious. As I listened to Jim tell me the story, I realized Jim's experience had transformed him to another level of service that would continue to bless many people. In fact, when he shared the story with me, it made me realize why he has been a blessing to so many people that have come through his business. Jim did not give up!

My hope is that whatever you are going through in your life, perhaps as I did, you might be able to reflect on the story of Job for encouragement realizing these eight points 1).You are not the first to go through it; 2).You will certainly not be the last to go through it, but more importantly, despite how you may feel in the current situation; 3). You are not alone; 4). God always has a plan even if you don't see it immediately; 5). Part of that that plan is for you and I not to give up; 6). Totally trust God; 7). God does not waist his trials and tribulations on people God does not plan to use; 8). God loves you.

When you have a sincere relationship with the Lord and are willing to walk with him unconditionally, only then will you understand GIVING UP IS NOT AN OPTION!

REFERENCES

1. Jaime Herndon; What is Preeclampsia? (2015) http://www.healthline.com/health/preeclampsia

2. Holy Bible KJV; Job Chapter 1: 1-22; Chapter 2:9-10.
   Thomas Nelson, Inc. (1976) PP.816; PP.817

3. Case Reports in Oncological Medicine
4. Volume 2013 (2013), Article ID 129813, 4 pages
5. http://dx.doi.org/10.1155/2013/129813

6. Renal Medullary Cancer in a Patient with Sickle Cell Trait

Narendrakumar Alappan,[1] Creticus P. Marak,[1] Amit Chopra,[1] Parijat S.Joy,[2] Olena Dorokhova,[3] and Achuta K. Guddati[4]

[1] Division of Pulmonary and Critical Care Medicine, Montefiore Hospital, Albert Einstein College of Medicine, Yeshiva University, New York, NY, USA

[2] Department of Internal Medicine, University

of Iowa Hospital, University of Iowa, Iowa, IA, USA

[3] Department of Pathology, Montefiore Hospital, Albert Einstein College of Medicine, Yeshiva University, New York, NY, USA

[4] Department of Internal Medicine, Massachusetts General Hospital, Harvard Medical School, Harvard University, 50 Fruit Street, Boston, MA, USA

Received 21 June 2013; Accepted 31 July 2013

Academic Editors: J. M. Buchanich and F. A. Mauri

7. Holy Bible KJV; Isaiah Chapter 26: 3. Thomas Nelson, Inc. (1976) PP.1052

8. Doctor Peter Grimm; Prostate Results Study Group; Prostate Specific Antigen (PSA); (2014) http://www.pctrf.org/prostate-specific-antigen-psa

9. Hughes, Ginnett, Curphy; Leadership Enhancing The Leeson's Of Experience 5th Edition McGraw Hill (2006) PP.79

SCRIPTURES OF ENCOURAGEMENT

(NKJV)

- Christians encourage each other – 1st Thessalonians Chap 4. Vs 18; Hebrews Chap 10. Vs. 24-25.

- Jesus Provides comfort – Mathew Chap 14. Vs 27

- God encourages us – 2nd Corinthians Chap 7. Vs 6

- God's word encourages us – Psalms Chap 119. Vs 28

- Adversity builds endurance – Romans Chap 5. Vs 3-4; James Chap 1. Vs 3

- God gives rest to the weary – Jeremiah Chap 31. Vs 25

- Those who hope the lord shall renew their strength – Isaiah Chap 40. Vs 31

- God will never forsake you – Hebrews Chap 13. Vs 5-6

- Know weapon formed against you will prosper – Isaiah Chap 54. Vs 17

- The lord helps those who follow him – 2nd Chronicles Chap 16. Vs 9

ABOUT THE AUTHOR

Charles Moorer Jr. is a graduate of Kent State University and Baker College. He is a dedicated father, husband, pastor, musician and leadership mentor currently based in Indianapolis, IN. Together with his band, The Faithful Few, Charles works diligently and faithfully to inspire people from all walks of life to live with purpose, love, and the peace of Christ.